THE HIERARCHY OF SHEEP

John Kinsella: bibliography

BOOKS

The Frozen Sea (Zeppelin Press, 1983)
The Book of Two Faces (PICA, 1989)
Night Parrots (Fremantle Arts Centre Press, 1989)
Eschatologies (FACP, 1991)
Full Fathom Five (FACP, 1993)
Syzygy (FACP, 1993)
The Silo: A Pastoral Symphony (FACP, 1995; Arc, UK, 1997)
Erratum/Frame(d) (Folio/FACP, 1995)
The Radnoti Poems (Equipage, UK, 1996)
Anathalamion (Poetical Histories, UK, 1996)
The Undertow: New & Selected Poems (Arc, UK, 1996)
Lightning Tree (FACP, 1996)
Graphology (Equipage, UK, 1997)
Genre (prose fiction, FACP, 1997)
Poems 1980-1994 (FACP, 1997; Bloodaxe Books, 1998)
The Hunt and other poems (FACP/Bloodaxe Books, 1998)
Grappling Eros (stories, FACP, 1998)
The Kangaroo Virus Project, with Ron Sims (Folio/FACP, 1998)
Visitants (Bloodaxe Books/FACP, 1999)
The Benefaction (Equipage, UK, 1999)
Wheatlands, with Dorothy Hewett (FACP, 2000)
The Hierarchy of Sheep (Bloodaxe Books/FACP, 2000)

AS EDITOR

The Bird Catcher's Song (Salt, 1992)
A Salt Reader (Folio/Salt, 1995)
Poetry (Chicago) – double issue of Australian poetry
   (with Joseph Parisi, USA, 1996)
Landbridge: Contemporary Australian Poetry (FACP/Arc, 1999)

JOHN KINSELLA

THE
Hierarchy
OF
Sheep

BLOODAXE BOOKS

ISBN: 1 85224 552 2

First published 2000 by
Bloodaxe Books Ltd,
Highgreen,
Tarset,
Northumberland NE48 1RP,

and published simultaneously in Australia
by Fremantle Arts Centre Press.

Bloodaxe Books Ltd acknowledges
the financial assistance of Northern Arts.

Cover printing by J. Thomson Colour Printers Ltd, Glasgow.

Printed in Great Britain by
Cromwell Press Ltd, Trowbridge, Wiltshire.

*Dedicated to Paul Keating
for the 'Redfern Speech'
and his support for the arts
in Australia*

Acknowledgements

Acknowledgements are due to the editors of the following publications in which some of these poems first appeared: *The Age*, *The Australian*, *Canberra Times*, *Cordite*, *Imago*, *London Review of Books*, *Newcastle Poetry Prize Anthology 1997*, *Oxford Poetry*, *Pequod*, *Poetry* (Chicago), *Poetry Ireland*, *Poetry Review*, *Richmond Review*, *Sunday Times*, *Sydney Morning Herald*, *Tabla*, *The Times Literary Supplement*, *Tinfish* and *TriQuarterly*. Some poems also appeared in the collections *Counter-Pastoral* (Vagabond Press, 1999), *Fenland Pastorals* (Prest Roots, 1999) and *Wheatlands*, with Dorothy Hewett (FACP, 2000), as well as in a booklet of poems published by the Fitzwilliam Museum, Cambridge relating to historical figures in their collection.

Contents

Adaptation

The chemical body
shielded by foliage
plays havoc with the seasonal
turnaround, the adaptational
quirks of vampire finches
on a small island
of the Galapagos
archipelago. Some species
just won't quit while
they're ahead, damning
definitive statements
for another stab
at fame. Never staying
that way long, loving
others' histories
vicariously, aspects
of warmth and personality
drawing tropical plants
in English hothouses,
dripping sweat and gloating
as a thin film of snow
coats the lawn. Through the glass
deciduous trees don't adapt
that fast – there's more or less
snow than last year.
And the bird sounds that permeate
aren't right and the light
contradicts asymmetrically:
the warmth inside so precise,
a dense Wet, a cloying
measure of precision.
Only a problem with a boiler
or a technician's indecision
will trigger the natural disaster
that will lead to adaptation.

After Sir Lawrence Alma-Tadema's *94° in the shade* (1876)

(for Peter Porter)

THYRSIS:

> *'Sit down now, goatherd, (think the Nymphs had asked you)*
> *And play your pipe, here where the hillside steepens*
> *And tamarisks grow on the slope. I will watch your goats.'*
> THEOCRITUS, 'Idyll 1'

The country in summer. The temperature hovers
    around the low thirties –
it is something of a heat wave. The surrounding
fields are tawny gold, though green tinges are almost
    tactless within a world
contracted to the killing jar. Unseen birds fuse,
tarnish with a chemical sky. Sullen trees wreck

the view so it's photosensitive. Animals
    twitch beneath the herbage.
Landscape and portrait hang languidly about each
other. In the foreground a youth is spread out cheek-
    in-hand, reading a book
on butterflies. His weapon – the butterfly net –
lies in front of him. He is confident. Maybe

overconfident. He's wearing an ivory
    summer suit with pith hat;
schoolboy on holidays, resting in the still shade,
confident within the granary of empire, wealth
    that keeps home secure.
Butterflies from other spaces congregate. Stooks
have been gathered, but lie in casual disarray.

Hockney's *Doll Boy* at the Local Country Women's Association Annual Musical: Wheatbelt, Western Australia

Opening night. As the curtain lifts
Doll Boy hovers in the wings,
the Town Hall full as the star drifts

centre-stage and in a falsetto sings
to the roar of the crowd –
the CWA already counting the takings

as the chorus of footy stars makes a loud
entry – smeared make-up and wigs,
ill-fitting blouses, the odd shroud-

length dress. A farmer digs
a mate in the ribs – that strapping
girl's my son, the last vestiges

of his reserve dissipating
with the electricity of the occasion.
At interval, the cast is buzzing

with excitement, taking slices of melon
from Doll Boy's chipped green plate,
blowing him kisses, calling him 'Queen'.

You're just not cute enough to rate
a place among us! Doll Boy, eyes
to himself, begins to create

a space apart, beyond the cries
of the crowd, the taste of melon on his lips:
sweet pink crystals bristling like stars,

full and sweet. And he grips
the memory of the vine – intricately
binding the patch near the roses and strips

of everlastings, ripening rapidly,
drinking the dam's muddy water insatiably,
preparing to feed the elect, delicately.

Local Forecast

the star dogs the moon
the rope is difficult to untwist
commotion is a borrowed day
in summer; the air clarified
bells are heard distantly
before rain dampens the effect

wicken fen

the surge in the cut of sedge light
as rusted dusk behind its cloak
comes in quickly, nomenclature of water
sullies and the mill is still, arms stretching
nowhere, the prey-bird eyeing the hide
in the bleached dead wood, a stoat stretching out
as the dead song sings it wasn't there

The Leech Barometer

'Dios sobre todo'

The artery forms a half-moon
like a leech against the surface
of your skin, transparent
despite the thickening darkness

each beat of the heart
pumps this sucker up, bold
as brass – wicked kris waiting
to cut its way out, sold

on love and the language
of the exotic, as if to hook
a wanton romantic –
tempestuous liver fluke

that apes the spirit,
mouth the colour of the sun,
eye like a swollen cloud,
fertile as prediction.

Bonfire Night

hot florets kick the air
and splash against the black
molecules crack in waves
as if there's no other light
about – colour, naming names
with hostile lips,
willing the rain to stay away,
as through the fens
fire lures blood-trill and wraith-talk,
an archaeological urge to placate
and incite, to listen close-at-hand,
distantly assuming a place
in this unearthing
of all that burns

Weeping Willow

You've seen this light before –
not often –
intermittently.

Saturated light through which boats
move sluggishly – sail, screw, oars, pole –

with banks labyrinths
or cloisters, or the walls
of a vein.

And a weeping willow, its somnolent
vapours anaesthetising the landscape,
clamping water and vessel,

lulling
the scene.

Yew Berry

Eye dangling on a twist of nerves,
phonetic, gelatinous package
rounded by gravity, pit
that cores, kernel of truth
seeing indifferently –
it's a joke, a bluff, a lure
to drag you in as if being a bird
is what it's about – luke-red
cushion against the topiary
stack or bollard, crazy horse
bristling and flicking
in the fading light
as you slip on jam
and a bland scent guides
you nowhere, despite
the demographics
being sticky with residue
of elsewhere, as acrid fumes
fill the gaps in memory
and incite the bird – suddenly –
to take the berry,
the sound of flight,
the volatility just below
the skin – ejective, implosive,
contingent

Mushrooming

'Out there...' out there where sheep dung
collates and top-dressed soil exudes
decomposing nitrogen, where under-rings
filigree networks of sensitivity
uneasy as roundup drifts from firebreaks
and first rains stimulate filaments;
where THE LAND does its urge thing,
conscious of literary precedent,
all that nudge and mystery
and primal aching: *clair de lune*,
the push-button radio astronomy
with calling occupants precision
in the blur of the between-seasons
evening – and yes, I'm afraid they DO believe it;
and yes, pink and grey and loud despite
a chill setting in: you know what *we've*
been reading. So, mushrooms
stem-severed and bagged, gills riddled
with field krill, rise to the less-pressured
waters, that is, out of the light-starved
trenches, rotting in sacks already bruised.
The disc plough wastes no time
before cutting in, breaking systems
of mycelium, night growth and industry.
Decay feeds and is bled: the freelancing
narratology of marketing boards.

Fenceposts

Grain has sprouted in the combed top
of the weather-scored fencepost – a slight crop
of green against the yellow backdrop –

the sandy soil taking brief rains
way down deep into the reservoir that drains
when wells are tapped, that strains

to fuel taproots of trees that fall
when you need a fencepost. But the wind's drawl
through interlock wire and steel eyelets, speared soil

firm around the star picket lashed
to the rickety fencepost, mean things have changed
around here. If you push soft palmskin, scratched

by days of driving stakes and twisting wire,
onto the needles of the old fencepost – not so hard as to puncture –
a burning sensation will spread and aspire

towards the visual points of the brain.
A Tom Roberts painting becomes a lost refrain –
information breaking up, the field enclosed – without gain.

Termites vein deadwood – tattoowork

Termites vein deadwood – tattoowork
some have called it. A sheep skull shattered
& sculpted into the shape of a parrot
crashed or brought down suddenly.

A plume of orange fungus gives a dead
stump a taste of the ludicrous, looking
almost vivacious in the strobe light,
plumped against the salty tesserae.

They search for something. A teapot
rust-blue & pocked with a tight grouping
of bullet holes. One of them can even
guess the calibre – triple two. Another

discovers the sound a southerly
makes as it rips through branches
high overhead. The shed skin of a dugite
is found caught in a fork of deadwood

close to the ground, & they check
to see if the owner hasn't returned.
Empty cartridge cases lie like hollow
notions as the conversation idles –

a kerosene tractor – just brass
pressings & not icons or talismans
worth preserving as memories,
as tools to shape narrative

when back inside they drink beer
        & watch TV.

Shoes once shod in a blacksmith's shop

Shoes once shod in a blacksmith's shop
rust on hooves lying on the rough edge
        of a paddock, horse skeletons
mingle with broken hoppers & elevators
& the iron-ringed wheels of surface strippers –
        sprouted grain thick on the
ground, like chemically stimulated hair.

The warped screens of a seed cleaner
buried to the knees in clay and salt, snake their
        way up towards the stunted fruit trees'
low-slung fruit like apodal spirits in a venomous
light – winter at their heels. Inside the shed
        the bellows groan in their frame
of blackbutt & mudbrick, the coal for the fire-

box lies scattered like shoddy talismans,
& the anvil sits sullenly, a dead loadstone.

Thornproof Tyres for a Pushbike

My brother is buying
a set of thornproof tyres.

You need them where he lives –
double-gees everywhere,
emerging out of paddock
and bitumen, rich
and poor soil alike.

In the past he placed
new tubes inside old tubes
cut to fit – a double layer –
with an injection of pepper
to plug the punctures
as the wheels turned.

But farm remedies
are only temporary – those
double-gees bristling like the spikes
police set at road blocks,
to bring high-speed chases
to a halt.

The spin of a double-gee, skull-hard
and compact, reaching out
as nettles do here;
tearing chunks out of the soles
of footwear, poisoning blood

and firebreaks – the stubble
yellow-ochre in a light
that should be harsher
than it is. It's all surfaces,
hiding residues of spray
and genetically modified crops,

but easily ruptured;
the bright burst of canola
coming on as the seasons advance,
the intensification of double-gees
already spread across the entire field –
swelling and setting root –

swelling and setting root –
the purchase of brand-name
lab-tested factory-produced
thornproof tyres made essential:
chemicals working the centrifuge,
filling holes as fast

as they are made, as fast
as my brother can ride.

There are places they won't go

There are places they won't go,
places they'll lose an acre or two
by keeping a safe distance, the crop
edgy and frayed where discs
didn't dig deep or where the seeder
ran out of super and grain, denuded boxes
like black holes drawing on each other's emptiness,
wheel-kick on loam-clod as the tractor
struggles to pull the machine
the hell out of there, though almost
wanting to be close – bright parrots
sarcastic in fruit trees, saying 'it's fine over here,
the fruit is good'. But they know better,
it's a patch to be avoided, old house
boarded up, water tanks rusted through.
'What a waste,' says an outsider. The reply:
'Brings a glow to the rest of the place.'
The shame hidden there, the bulk
of the farm productive, well-managed.

Autumn landscape

The trees might refuse
to throw their leaves,
hanging onto them through winter,
chilling birds as if time has nothing
to do with life – dark blue sky
as dark as storm-black night,
absorbing gold from lifeless
embers, ghost limbs
as solid as ground
smouldering like riches –
trapped glare of summer,
the grass losing its sibilance.

Early Morning

foxes printing marshy ground
between house and barn
flickering like neurosis in the ute's
headlights under late moonlight
and everywhere deflections
from frost building its elaborate deposits –
neighbours' kids thinking
about rusty traps found in sheds
set along roadsides, jaws
cold as sheep bones cast over paddocks,
divining a bitter end

Ice

It's so clear you touch the surface
only half-expecting resistance,
but your tepid flesh sticks
and beneath its hard clear finish
the stuff of puddles is sharp
and laid out perfectly – a leaf,
brown and crinkled residue of autumn,
tense and precious. Beneath
it might be a perfect climate.
Further down the path, shattered
sheets of ice disperse reflection:
your face, a branch, the stark
blue winter sky. A landscape
saturated with trigonometries.
Small tundras refusing reverence,
exteriors you might slide across
or fall through endlessly.

hydrography

Obsessive reservoir ringing changes as dowser & hazel twig twist
sharply over water-way deep patterning flood plain mimicking a
subterranean hot spot in dry southern places damping family &
stock & seasons of poise designated drought or stream riveting
bodies of water perennial corpses diminishing a Pont Neuf flurry
of mechanics as the gaudy fountain sprays fashionable names in-
font per vascular *fons et origo*, georgically gloating weir a misshapen
picaresque fattened on bloodworms scripted on **tidal flats** innate
down-stream, filaments flexing circularities & principles, beauty-
flow bent theatrical, red perch destroying status quo, changing
habitats feeding arterial pumps as empire drives its barge inwards
from the mouth, large-bellied black swan duping a wader's scurry
compressing slurry occupation like stacks in hyper-spatial flocks;
text block on text block opening engravings from *Les Raisons des
forces mouvantes*: confluence, text & pre-history, editorials inciting
offshore enquiries into Cayman Island companies.

a rose is a rose is a rose is a rose

From Rose Hill the town
is both large and small –
it is a thing of the eye
and there's nothing complex
about it: a flock of white cockatoos
implodes to a point of singularity,
before pluming out over the football field,
town hall, a stand of trees
without a name. It's the paradox
of place: always the variety,
the pleasant conflict of styles.
The rose, the cockatoo,
the failure of colour as whiteness
merges with sunlight.

Fallow

They'll leave this field fallow –
Good land while nothing grows.

Not long after burning
A father dropped and was buried.

Without markings and eroded
By extremes it wasn't called a grave.

Later ploughed, nothing came
To the surface – but by then

A different people owned it and ignorant
Of its history *might* have glimpsed

The chunky bones of livestock,
The fine bones of a marsupial,

And thought little of it. But the old family,
Having bought it back, have traced

A genealogy, and family anecdotes
Draw them to a place the size

Of a football field. Anonymity and time
Have made the father – the father's father –

As large as memory, potentially rich
As a field that's fallow.

After Pumping

In summer when the day
burns its way through weeks
and months, and the rain gauge
collects sediments of dust,

and evenings are cowls
of super-heated light
cooled to tepid night,
the sprinklers

dowse the lawn
in ochre water forced
up from the dam
by the snarling pump;

amongst the paddocks'
fading yellows and browns,
an indelible lawn
cools the mind.

The pump coughs
and fills with silence,
and deadwood flickers
along the fenceline –

the tawny frogmouth
moves with caution,
always away from
the green incursion.

Rainwater Tanks – Summer

Steel moulds sledgehammered into place
and the mesh bone structure holding
the hard grey flesh; or the elevated cylinders
corrugated like ripples in clear water
stagnated and laid over each other –
perched high on metal gantries
or ground hugging of broad circumference
anchored on a bed of railway sleepers,
rings to be tapped as the water level
brings the reverberations
down an octave – the atoms
less excited, the sound cooler –
echoing nowhere as the sun
high in the sky heats the silver skin
like a furnace; or down to the standpipe
in the old dodge, running a load
of scheme water (the canvas pipe
quivering like a reed instrument
before gushing indifferently) back
to the dangerously low rainwater tanks,
the treated liquid mingling with the tepid
dregs of roof-gathered rainwater. A dog
cools itself in a decommissioned tank,
lid peeled back like a knife-opened can,
congealed hessian for a bed,
raising a snout to take in the hot air
in brief snorts, knowing where the water
is: the brass spigots holding
back every drop, despite the moving
parts, gravity, and a corrosive thirst.

Uncle Clem reckons quite a few

Uncle Clem reckons quite a few
of the trees struck in forest
country around these parts
are marri & that when they
are struck an explosion
follows, blowing large
splinters of wood in all
directions. He says
no one is really sure
why this happens
but that it might
have something to do
with the water-filled tree cells
expanding rapidly!
On those occasions
when Jarrah is struck
it tends to lose a strip of timber
from strike point to ground.
Sometimes surrounding trees
will die but only those nearby.

Rainwater Tank

Half full in winter
Half empty in summer.

Take care in the long grass

Take care in the long grass
the long dry summer grass
in this zone of dugites and gwarders
even a stray tiger snake
take care your gaiters
are strapped tight
or that denim is double-thickness
and tucked tight into boot tops
bridled with burrs,
resistant to the strike,
latch and puncture,
hot as hell sweating, prickling
and saying damn-it-all, give me thongs,
and a tourniquet and a bottle of Condy's Crystals
and a mouth that'll latch on and suck venom
out like death IS love; long grass rustling
brittle fabric like wings on insects
enough to lift you out of the thick of it,
high as the soul need go
to escape dugite, gwarder,
errant tiger snake out from the dank
fringe of swamp,
the long grass,
the nomenclature of poison
and body

Deciduous?

The she-oaks have dropped their needles
and a crop-duster flies against popularity;
    a new cache of seedlings for land reclamation
is sitting pallet-bound in the paddock
    while nearby an overhead petrol tank leaks.

The phone rings in a house a long way from here
    but I can't hear it, I paint mental portraits
to take back and adapt to my own purpose. Even
drums of spray are photogenic. Here, a blush
    signals the onset of flu or the body
correcting an emotional oversight in another place.

The rank-and-file collect at powerpoints,   ·
    light as constant here as in the city,
less storm of fire interrupting the flow – but
this can happen anywhere. Gone the slow
    but comforting cough of the petrol-driven
generator and the feeble globes. Nightlight
and daylight meant something really different
    then. Fear came with this weakness
though confidence came with independence.

The light-switches stuck on the ceiling
    grin as we come in for the evening meal,
strings hanging like nooses set for sheep thieves
who leave fleeces strung over the fences.

White cockatoos lift in plumes and split

White cockatoos lift in plumes and split,
carried back to each other like mercury –
the town rangers breaking the surface tension
as the cull begins and white spray
is a celebration of 'everything in moderation'...
a scheme-watered wandoo is lost, white
and seething in the bright light of late Autumn,
uncomfortable clouds off-centre,
sagging over the folds of Mount Bakewell.
In deciding upon a plot for a fading aunt
the lost grave of a miscarriage is discovered.
Up Ensign Dale Court pink and grey galahs
twist on the rough grey bark of a York gum.
It's an access lane between properties
but the threat of a road seems distant.
Ensign Dale broke this zone open
at the time of the incursion. Another species
of parrots beheads roses on the hill.
The garden is richly scented and death
seems nowhere. It signifies nothing.
And yet, the cemetery is a tourist attraction
and the business of death goes on, respectfully.

Rich soil, the mechanism: a farm is sold

Deep in the Valley rich soil drives
the mechanism. Grain spills from the husks.
Despite the season of recovery,
the family is forced to sell up –
a lost century becomes a dynasty
and the rich soil becomes polluted.
They've cleared and shaped the place,
a portrait of themselves.
On a summer evening they'll
look out over the paddocks,
over burnt stubble, over stands of mallee,
through a flock of sulphur-crested
cockatoos, into the rich red sunset.
They'll leave to slaps on the back and sympathy
and the words, 'It's a hard place – beautiful
but unforgiving.' Their sorrow is understood.
The farm will be deserted for a time
as if the market is stronger
than the salt-eaten roots of fence posts,
whose coils of wire unravel chaotically,
or stronger than contour banks arcing out like circuitry –
signals breaking up, eroding with winter,
lacking design. Rich soil
drives the mechanism.

They visit their graveyards – family,
machinery, sheep – now genderless
the land struggles for identity –
'she'll be right' loses its echo
and runs into the past, a nickname
becomes another entry in the Domesday book
along with echidna tiger-snake tawny frogmouth
commodities futures tare gross barometer.
Rich soil drives the mechanism.

Salmon gums bloom topheavy like oracles
with too much to say and the fox adjusts
to the climate generation by generation.
In the Paddock of the Killers
the spectres of slaughtered sheep graze, the knife
blunts in an otherwise empty kitchen.
Wrought iron scrollwork downloads
onto the surface which is already showing
more than a dusting of salt
which has emerged from somewhere deep,
from before the clearing, from before Settlement
when land made its own investments
and the mechanism hadn't begun
its renaming, before this became a place
where the spirit has been stripped back
like spent paint and whitewashed over.
Bright birds are still with evening.
Residue collects in the gulleys.
Speculators cross the boundaries
and test for fertility. Rich soil
drives the mechanism.

Rhizomic Perth

(for Frances Harvey, student of architecture)

In creating a language of Edge
check below the surface – harness
the stuff that drives colloquial bric-a-brac,
unearth interned histories, pay lip-service
to the death of serpents. You've been there,
so you know how the sand swirls at the base
of the Scarp, how the Hills cradle the alternative
arts – the storm-felled timbers, open
living spaces, while down in the suburbs
display homes put on a brave front –
liberty, fraternity, and equality.
Only God knows how close the French were –
and the climate so Mediterranean!
But with all that salt water and it being
a hell-of-a-long-way from anywhere,
they eye catchment areas nervously,
and wish there were more rivers to dam.
The talk is of desalination as the ocean
makes beautiful waves and aches under
the carcinogenic sun – rippling like a visiting
rock band from New York or London.
Petrol stations hover over water mounds.
The Kimberley pipeline is a broken thread
of hansard, and the Swan River constantly
changes shape – a riverside development,
new freeway. Facadism plants roots deeper
than impact, and the cbd's silver towers
glimmer like advertisements. In Northbridge
the police patrol the parks. Date stones
shine. Surveillance cameras integrate.
A Nyungar community centre keeps
its gates locked. Respectable firms deploy
Federation verandahs, local timbers,
and skylights. The odd glass pyramid crops
up here and there. The Roundhouse
sees off the Fremantle Doctor, Rottnest
plays host to a convention. The Old Brewery

footnotes King's Park – an open and closed case –
we ARE closer to nature, despite the traffic lights,
as the war-dead of Perth declare
their independence, as Mrs Dance
transforms into a tree.

Sun, Sun, Sun, Sun...

They say that my skin is sensitised,
that Australia would certainly bring out
the worst in me – an exile of the surface,
blemish that explodes below,
disorganising tissue and seeding
blood – each gesture
of growth a piece of legislation –
ownership under the bright lights
of Canberra, State capitals,
body politic, passport offices,
– terra nullius – primogeniture,
collusion of Irish and English
ancestors, biopsies and visas,
like some new home out of the sun,
genetically modified, comfortable
in artificial light.

Displacement
(for Gail)

The rush of ibises in the late afternoon
unsettles the heat – as if humidity
were character building, busy
'naturing nature'. Air and water
parody each other. At night
the grid of lights is tactile,
and the eye senses every twitch
of the luminous: a late hazy moon rises
suddenly, shrugging off darkness,
as if there's tension between
the enamelled city and acrylic foliage
hanging heavy over King's Park.
Each tree – a totem for a dead soldier –
shivers with the humidity: widow makers
that might drop a limb and take out
a brace of lovers, fill the dark
untouchable part of a river
that we've systematically emptied.
A chemi-luminescence
mimics a ferry's lights as it trails
towards South Perth. Darkness
intensifies, forcing biographies:
it is said, it is held, it diverges.

Sublimated through our thought

You reconstruct your past
through ads in weekend liftouts
or the odd Australian novel
that finds its way onto an English shelf,
assuming the subject-matter 'Australian',
which is a safe assumption to make.
A warm day, a sharp frost,
a stretch of empty moorland in the North,
might prompt your 'memory'.
As farm machinery invests and dissects
the peaty soil of the fens
the reddish clay of the past
turns to dust or puddles like vats
of blood during flood. You pick up
on hearsay in a local pub,
or an aboriginal myth reconstructed
by an educational publisher,
'sublimated through our thought'.
What remains the same
no matter the place, is the gutted sheep,
the dogs among the entrails.
Though the heat intensifies
exposure.
            A cousin rides her horse
out to the blokes working
the Hundred Acres, their tucker
cool in her saddle bags.
Space is expansive and concentrates
her gender. Aborigines stook in families
and one of the white blokes
jokes about wine flagons turning to water,
he thinks his laughter pristine and expansive,
brilliant enough for any locality.
In the fens dialect is lampooned
and a bunch of lads sings karaoke,
forgetting their prejudices.
Somewhere, the Concorde
breaks the sound barrier
and modernity instils itself
as memory, an afterthought.

Interim

Managing the casual moments between art theatres
& roof gardens, between vanity & epistles
dragged out of the Australian war wounded,
glory strung up like a gaudy yew tree, berries
rampant like eyes popped from the skull of a critic,
the hedgehog works hard on keeping a low profile
at the back door of discussion, the garrulous light
painful to his nightbound eyes aching beneath
spiky brows. They don't trust him, & he's
not so sure himself. Eventually they'll throw
open the door & march out – but they won't
crush him, just leave him there alone & wondering.

Ode to Abigail

Abigail
did the first full frontal
on Australian television
before being snuffed out
by the pantyhose strangler
on Number 96 –
I hid behind the couch
and watched
as my mother and Jackie
said 'well what do you expect';
a couple of years earlier
another TV star had taken
my mother's racing-car-driver boyfriend
after being sprung on his arm
at the Channel 7 Christmas Ball –
mum went on to Uni, Abigail
slipped into mum's old copywriting job
as we watched the man in the drip-dry suit
keep jumping off Barrack Street jetty,
mum's last commercial

On Looking Outside Judith Wright's 'Request to a Year'

When the generator went down and the storm was at its height she forgot her eldest son and his father stuck miles away in a neighbour's paddock, their open-topped tractor struggling with the disc plough in the heavy soil, spotlights like planets tossed from their orbits, roguely elliptical between the gravities of fences, trees, and untamable land forms. She'd been with them as the light grew dim and hesitated, realising too late that she'd forgotten to refuel when she'd struggled to throw the crank handle, feeling its mule-kick as it fired up. As it went dark and her isolation burnt with the intense and instant illumination of lightning strikes, like an over-exposed negative the room caught in its perfect order, she recalled reading Judith Wright's 'Request to a Year' and thinking it strange that the woman could have remained so removed from the scene. But the realisation that she was alone in that house and her son was with his father cast doubts on the great-great-grandmother's apparent indifference. She considered the pain in her shoulder from starting the generator, the children she'd lost in childbirth. She considered how brilliantly the lightning highlighted those parts of the picture that could never be illuminated by the best-tended and strongest of generators. Like an x-ray she saw her blood flow within her own skin. Out there, in the paddock, two skins held their own blood and the flow between them was only imagined.

Il faut cultiver notre jardin

Cleared land is a place of weeds,
bee-wings' razored whirr
and a cut trunk hollowed
by white ants – a font
beneath swabs of cloud.

When sunlight cordons
off an area for display,
hill-clefts and ravines
resist, retaining shadow.
Small birds sing and you

don't think of their name,
the air-drag of crows' wings
just overhead. Jam
trees keep their sap
tight beneath the bark.

Late winter warmth
dries cushions of moss,
rapidly brittle and crumbling
around purple sprays
of Paterson's Curse;

onion grass cuts low weather
and twenty-eights are caught
in a pause, a cessation
of dialogue – instruments
poised about the developing fruits

of the creek canopy.
Working their tails, chests
puffed and springing angles
like hearts, claws hooked
as numbers in a code

that won't quite scan:
but neither does god!
A globe-bodied spider
concentrates a poison
that bothers only flies,

mosquitoes and ants;
the sun intensifies and parrots
are burnt to silhouettes,
a clear night with frost threatens,
plants folding like prayer.

Figures in a Paddock

In their wake the furrows,
partings in long grass,
burrs hell-darning their socks
like recovered memories.

Parallel to the fence – star pickets
mark depth, interlock mesh
letting the light and visuals
through, keeping the stock

in or out – like religious tolerance.
Down from the top-road to the creek,
arms akimbo, driven against
insect-noise, a breeze that should

be rustling up a performance.
Towards the dry bed, marked
by twists and shadow-skewed
river-gums, bark-texture

runs to colour like bad blood.
The sky is brittle blue,
foliage thin but determined:
colour indefinable beyond green.

They walk, and walking makes history.
And tracks. All machinery.
The paddock inclines. A ritual of gradients.
Ceremony. Massacre. Survey.

Hectic Red

Quartz sparks randomly
on the pink and white crust
of the salt flats, spread out
beyond the landing,
where bags of grain –
wheat and oats
in plastic and hessian –
lips sewn shut,
packed tight, flexing dust
and dragging their feet
to the edge, are tipped
onto the truck – feed-
grain, filling out
the flat-top, another body sack
waiting to be fed,
from top to bottom,
the sheep hollow-gutted
in the long dry, green-feed
deficient and this
the diminishing stock
of back-up tucker;
the best paddocks
up beyond the salt
all hoofed and bitten,
stray tufts targeted
and levelled,
dry roots crumbling
and dropping to dried-out
stream-beds beneath,
so no new encrustations
of salt emerge back down
in the low places, just the old crust,
pinking off – at night,
the crazy pick-ups
spinning wheels
and throwing headlights,
the bonnets rising and falling
in choppy waves, the light
as unstable as a camera

and the darkness dropping in
like black sacking; bleak rabbits
dashing about,
their blood infra,
the forecast – hectic red.

Wind Sock

Double-gees littered
the old runway like
anti-personnel mines –
tiny steer skulls
camouflaged between
a taut blue sky
and the reddish strip
of compressed earth.
As the plane circled
overhead,
the wind sock
lingered impotently
beside an endless expanse
that suggested any specific
point of landing was a joke –
it looked safe to go down anywhere.
But a strange quirk of weather
known only to aviators
who originally laid down the strip
ripped the plane out
of its torpor, scattered
it among the double-gees
and primary colours;
the wind sock withering
from the heat
of impact.

Firebox

It angered him that she would call it the 'firebox' –
'It's a woodbox,' he'd say, filling it with offcuts
    from old railway sleepers
    and fence posts, storm-felled trees
and once-brilliant stands of blackbutt. He continued
to complain after she'd gone inside – 'a woodbox!'
    again and again – each
piece perfectly stacked, the box as full as it could be

before the lid came down. Returning the wheel-barrow
to the woodpile he glanced at the axe, considered
    the circular saw – this
    was his place. The woodbox
was where he and his wife met. He could see her clear
enough from the stack – moving around in the kitchen,
    hanging her batik cloth,
dye running like body fluids over the sink.

'It's not merely a hobby,' she would say over
and over, 'people pay good money – a hell of
    a lot more than the farm
    brings in. You'd do better
selling that bloody firewood in town than keeping
every fire in the house burning – those sparks flying
    up flues and over the
the tinder-dry paddocks'. He'd curse her and take to

a particularly hard piece of wood with his
splitter, the iron biting deep, fresh from grinder.
    He'd unpack the woodbox
    and devise ways of packing
yet more wood into its tin shell. 'Cutting, sawing,
splitting. Cutting, sawing, splitting.' Incendiary
    litany: fire fire fire –
warmth and light and food and security. Fire fire.

'The firebox refills as fast as I empty it,'
she sighs. He watches the patterns on her batik
    shirt as she drips wax. He
    sees a snake – a dugite –
in his mind's eye – it's coiled and burning at the core
of the woodpile. He unpicks the stack with thick gloves
    and pinches it firmly
behind the head – like on television. He sees

it in the woodbox which is half full. He sees
it inside and watches it slither down into the puzzle.
    Her body rejects the
    antivenin. Some years
later he remarries. His new wife stokes the fires.
The farm still runs at a loss but he is content.
    The batik curtains have
seen better days but he won't let this wife replace

them. They don't argue much. She's easy to get on
with, he thinks, splitting a thick chunk of salmon gum
    he'd driven an hour to
    pick up. The axe sings – it
has its own beauty. There are only small things that
niggle at him. She calls the woodbox a firebox.
    She worries about sparks.
But it's autumn now and warmth fills the house, their home.

Cut in Half by a Sheet of Corrugated Iron
Ripped from a Shed by a Strong Wind
(for Mark Rudman)

High wind and sunshine – sharp outline
against blurring odds, jacked
out of four-by-two
shed-beams
torn tap tap rip
galvanising nails
pinging out, force-9/doldrums
force-9/doldrums,
animals huddling
out in the open,
skin-lifting, dead boughs
dropping out in the habitat,
nest-fall and dissonance,
that sheet of corrugated
airmailed, kingsford smithed
into the flesh, earmarked
and with his name
written on it, old farmer
emerging from the shuddering
shithouse, porno mags
stacked up out there
beyond the memories of a dead wife,
cut down outside his prime,
ripple-edged dual-self,
blood-flagged in strong wind,
abstract to the end: 'didn't know
what hit him...'

The Hierarchy of Sheep – a report from my brother

1 *Rams*

To be lamb meat or castrated to wethers
or reign in longevity and fertility
and throw the shearer who can't afford
to hit back, golden balls hanging like trophies,
deep wrinkles genetically engineered
bringing the long merino wool as fine
as the buyer could want, as lambs
of an old ram with a kick so hard
that it takes a couple of roustabouts
to hold it down, will be as boisterous
and determined to take the world on –
'there is a lot of genetics in sheep,
even their temperament'.

A ram horns its way into the blue singlet
of a shearer and through to his belly,
coiled like the spiral matrix of hatred
recognising captivity – fly strike
thickening wool with goo and maggots,
possibly a rogue that's broken down fences,
furious amongst the ewes, savage to its fellows,
headbutting and cracking the competition –
the shearer wastes his enemy with a jet
of aero-start up the nostrils, abusing the farmer
for feeding the bastard lupins and lime
while he watches on nervously, fearing a vengeful shearer
as the feelers sense their way out of the sheath
of the ram's penis – cut by the handpiece
the ram is rendered 'useless',
unable to find the ewe's cunt.

All cut by a shearer at one time or another –
sewn together with dental floss or wearing their scars
gracefully beneath the new season's haute-couture,
role play as if gender has meaning out there –
collectively warding a fox from the lambs.
Earlier the farmer assisted a birth
and then shot a mother polluted by stillbirth –
utilitarian in the way of things. Months back
he'd joked as rams were unleashed
into a ripe flock; up with the crack of dawn,
watching the weather, noticing the comings
and goings of birds. Now rain threatens
and older ewes kick like hell,
all of them full with young, milk veins
up and pumping hard to udders –
somewhere a nick with a blade has a vein
knotted off with needle and thread,
the myth declaring that another takes its place.
'Sometimes ewes get nervous and sensing
their humility is not hard. They get this manic shake
and tears fall from the corners of their eyes.'
A lamb drops in a catching pen.
A shearer aims a teat at his mate
and squirts a shot of milk into his ear.
The shed is full of swearing and laughter.

3 *Wethers*

Low-maintenance power houses
scouring the goldfields for scant feed
their wool full of wool spiders, chewing
a shearer's singlet to extract salt
as the handpiece worms off a strip of flesh
and bleats come from somewhere deep
inside, wiry and up against it the farmer
keeping them on a slender thread
to boost the quality of wool – harsh
conditions producing fine strands.
A fly-struck wether with flesh
hanging in sheets and flies erupting
from its ribcage has a pesticide
sprayed into its cavities –
but not even this and the remnants
of testosterone can keep it upright
and a short while later the dull thud
of a gun being fired somewhere outside
moves contrapuntally into the shed,
teasing the buzz of the plant, downtubes whirring,
handpieces snatched in and out of gear.
Even the dead added to the tally.

4 *Lambs*

The assault comes on strong: tailed,
castrated, ringed, earmarked, and mulesed.
Tails gas-axed off. Alive and highly strung
and either moving on to weaner
then hogget then ram, ewe, or wether,
or consumed while the flesh is tender.

The Shooting Party

1.

It is harvest time. Temperatures are soaring towards 40 in the shade. The main room of the hut. Three bedrooms open onto it. It serves as kitchen, living room, etc. The shower is going in a room off stage. RALPH *is showering.* BILL, JACK *and* MICK *are sitting at the table. They've just knocked off work.*

JACK *(unlacing his boots)*
Well, I'd like to get some shooting in,
I've had enough of this fucking wheat bin.

MICK
Geez, it's hot. Fourth day the mercury's
Hit forty, that promised change is in no hurry.

JACK *(thumping Mick on the arm)*
You don't ever listen to me, do you
I said I'd like to get out there and bag a roo.

MICK *(rubbing his arm)*
Christ, it's all you ever talk about
And as I'm two foot away you don't need to shout.
I've told you time and time again
I'm not interested in you or your gun!

(Jack goes to thump Mick again but Bill blocks him.)

BILL
Come on mate, lay off, you've been
At him for days. Look, I'll mention
It to my ol' man down at the pub this evening
And see if we can't get some shooting
In later tonight. A few beers and we'll be
Among them. It's what we all need, a shooting party.

MICK
Well, count me out, it's not my scene.

52

JACK

You're coming you snotty-nosed little queen
If I have to drag you by the hair.

BILL

Come on Mick, just come out for a beer.
You don't have to shoot anything if you don't want to.

JACK

Hey, Ralph. Ralph! Fuck, he wouldn't have a clue.
Hey Ralph, turn that fucking shower off.

(The shower cuts out.)

RALPH *(offstage)*

What the hell do you want? It's a bit rough
When a bloke can't even take a shower
Without being harassed.

(Ralph appears in the room dripping wet with a towel wrapped around him.)

JACK

          Water
Everywhere!

RALPH

          Well, what do you want?

JACK

Want to come out tonight? A roo hunt.

RALPH

Sure. Haven't shot anything before.
Wouldn't mind giving it a go. Is it within the law?

(Jack whips Ralph's towel off. They wrestle and laugh.)

2.

Hotel. (Bill, coming back from the bar with a round of drinks.)

BILL

Not a problem. The ol' man will even give us
A carton of piss if we bag a dozen. Plus,
He'll let us use his pick-up. He's staying
In town tonight, reckons he'll be sinking
Half the grog they've got on tap. And Mick,
He says to tell you that when he brings a truck-
Load of feed-grade wheat for you to sample
On Monday, you're to praise it as an example
Of the finest premium grade to be found
In the district!

(Mick laughs uneasily.)

JACK

And if he doesn't he'll be six foot underground!

BILL

Hey, Jack, been trying to chat up Josie?
She tells me you won't leave up, coming to her all rosy-
Cheeked and smooth talking. Well, she thinks
You're a creep so if you want to keep the drinks
Flowing you'd better lay off. *(He laughs.)*

JACK

Bitch!

BILL

Come on boy, watch the language.

JACK

That's a bit rich
Coming from you! Only yesterday you called her a slut.

54

BILL

But I'm allowed to 'cause she's still hot
For yours truly. And who wouldn't be, a classy bit like me.

(Andy wanders over.)

ANDY

You're full of it, Withers. Want to be
A pretty boy like hairy here. *(He rubs Mick's hair.)* Hey, Jack
Want a game of pool? You can rack
Them up and break. Ten bucks to the winner.
Come on, you can afford to lose a tenner.

(They walk away.)

MICK

Can't stand that guy. He's as bad as Jack

RALPH

Don't let it get to you. They've just got a knack
Of rubbing people up the wrong way –
they've just got to have their say.

MICK

It's worse than that – they're malignant...
And you should know about that, being a medical student.

3.
Outside.

JOSIE
So what are you doing here if you're a vegetarian?

MICK

I don't know. I've got to live with them. It's a question
Of survival. You know, sometimes when there's a break
Between trucks I stare out into the paddock
Over the road and picture myself as a stalk
Of wheat just waiting for the header. But then I baulk
And think about how I've only got so many days

Before I get my pay and this will just be memories.
Has it ever struck you as strange that the crop
Closest to the bins is the last to be harvested, is the last drop
In an ocean that's been sucked dry?

JOSIE

Nothing here strikes me as unlikely. It's a dreary
But strange place. It's as if they speak and think
Another language. The rules are different. Too much drink
Probably. Sometimes I feel as if they're going
To punish me for thinking against them, that I'm wrong   .
And they're right. I can't really explain it, but it's
Something to do with the deep blue of the sky, it's
Something to do with the stale red of the soil.
And the heat pulls the liquid out of the soul.

MICK

But I reckon it's the outsiders that are the strangest.
It's as if they lose the plot trying to pass some test
They imagine they're expected to undergo. Take
Ralph for example, he was a reasonable sort of bloke
When he arrived, and now he's a loud-mouthed hoon
He sees his time here as some kind of initiation,
A rite of passage. That's why he's after you,
It's an attempt to prove his manhood. A screw
Is all he needs now he's been pissed and handled a gun.
I heard him last week joking about being a surgeon,
How he'd get to feel up women while they were anaesthetised.
Then he went on about cadavers, and though disguised
As humour, there was excitement in his eyes.
I find him more worrying than Jack or Andy's
Blatant aggression. You know exactly where you stand
With them, but with Ralph…

JOSIE

                                    I was Bill's girlfriend
For about six months. I trust him, though he's a pain.
Always trying to prove himself – it's a strain
Being with someone who has to be liked by everybody.

56

MICK

Yeah, Bill's okay, though we disagree
On just about every point. Listen. That's a gun being fired
In the distance. It's as if the sky is electrically wired
And a wisp of moisture has lifted from a creature
And sparked with the contact. And now the temperature's
Dropping. The night is growing cold. The change
Has arrived. The bin will close and a rusty mange
Will spread through the remaining harvest.
The season will linger on without being blessed.
There'll be no celebrations. Just dark murmurings
That'll fuel a vicious summer.

JOSIE

                              Look, there are rings
Around the moon.

MICK

                    Yes, a storm is brewing. Soon a wind
Will whip in from the south, and strip the moon down to the rind.
And then it will be blanketed in clouds thicker
Than topsoil. The blood of the dead will soak the core
Of this ransacked country.

JOSIE

                    Your talk is addictive.
Listen, I hear a vehicle. They're heading back. Be selective
With what you say. They'll be on a high.
I've seen it before. Something has to die
For them to find their inner selves. And it's ugly.
I've seen it before. Let's hide in this gully.

(The vehicle approaches. Mick lifts his head and looks straight into the spotlight. A shot is fired. Josie screams. Later she'll recall that it sounded like a .222.)

Sun, Unreturnable Gift: Composition with Pink & Grey Galahs in Flight

(for Kevin Hart)

The sun, unreturnable gift
obsesses the feature window,
as if the leaden clouds moving steadily
towards the point between occupancy
and delivery aren't even there

So here, in Cambridge, a composition
Sunday-afternoons itself into existence,
as if a photograph makes memory
an authentic exhibit: that the pink & grey
galahs in this photograph sent by

My mother, interring through
the hard lens that lets in light
and yet keeps the atmosphere out,
are permanently engaged
with the immanence of flight,

Flashes within the frame
which, like the sun, shine on
oblivious behind the cloud
now firmly in place, the birds fallen
from their upward rise from high perches,

Outside the memory of the camera
outside the season is distinctive
and the beeches reclothe with the sign:
    'Comme rupture franche
    Plutôt refoule ou tranche
    Les anciens désaccords
      Avec le corps'
as if each word is the perfect prayer,
and yes, I was there, and saw similar
birds fly within their hemisphere,

Though I took no photograph,
and if I had, would have lost it
to the sun, a gesture of return,
like the refoliation of evergreens
after locusts, flood, or drought.

Crossing a Stile at a Country Church in Summer, Western Australia

The steps between churchyard and rectory
neatly aspire, set-square apexed to keep
vestments from wire bloody with rust,
the ground baked like white pottery;

such a hot day – even morning prayers
evaporate, the cloth wet with perspiration
and then bone dry, like the wooden frame,
not quite leaving the ground, the stares

of tourists and non-believers; at the point
directly above the fence the minister
transmigrates – those Norfolk paths
of his childhood, his fading accent,

the passion and flame of belief buried deep,
the whole world tinder dry – just a spark
enough to make a fire in the mouth,
his words devouring the people as they sleep.

The Texture of Stubble

aloof and prim and proper
prompted up, on-end and spiking
haze hangover, as if a vacuum
is blue and has body, but never bristles
that rash or counterpoint, lift and shove
off-handedly, the months, as evening
shows the way, and cultural cross-
fertilisation is an ashen reflection
of marsupials and foxes in hot dens

Drugs and Country Towns

(for Paul Muldoon)

The SS Commodore with tinted windows
will make the run to Perth in a few hours,

the stereo flat-tack and the driver pumped up,
hanging out but intoxicated by the prospect

of picking up, the hollowness filled with bravado:
the deal better not fuck up or heads will roll.

A week's wages and a bunch of mates
who've put cash up front – the whole town

speeding off its face and strung out,
they'll be counting the hours

and tempers will flare, blokes
knocking girlfriends about,

bongs strained and beer on beer drained
to help them get through. The town is growing –

spreading out – out there ploughing,
listening to the call of the tawny frogmouth,

and then a run through the fast-food outlet.
Later, it's a mate's place for speed and videos.

Not yet big enough to hide rip-offs
those with contacts are jacking up the profits –

the chemists, forcing frowns back
as they sell fit-packs and dieting tablets,

are asked to fill city prescriptions.
The older blokes are mumbling

at The Club – 'one of them young blokes
shore two hundred the other day

and the next day couldn't finish a run...'
The cops are getting rough – stripping cars

and raiding farm houses. They
have their chosen ones – the boys

in the footy team, the girls who do favours.
The world grows small fast – the town

moves out to the farms. The drive-ins
have shut down and fast music

comes into the Country Hour
like Armageddon. On a back verandah

a farmhand says to his girlfriend:
'I love you...the sunset is magic.'

Three Triolets

Fetish

the vascular glow of she-oaks
offsets the loneliness and fear,
darkness between farmhouses soaks
the vascular glow of she-oaks –
intense residue that invokes
restlessness in your sixteenth year,
the vascular glow of she-oaks
offsets the loneliness and fear

Drought

a lack of water drives you to the well
deep below the burning surface
where unknown wheel-animalcules dwell;
a lack of water drives you to the well
to free sheep from drought's death-spell,
to drop a stone from the furnace,
a lack of water drives you to the well
deep below the burning surface

Adolescence on the backroads: crosses and flowers

on gravel roads cars slide further
and stretches of bitumen fuel
rollbacks and burnouts – laid rubber,
on gravel roads cars slide further
and licences don't matter,
the cops rarely out there; cut sick and duel,
stoked by alcohol – then the chapel,
on gravel roads cars slide further

Quails' Eggs

What was it that drew you into the cage,
gently shooing the quails away from sitting,
studying their small ground-hollow nests
and speckled eggs with care and patience,
canaries and finches nervous overhead –
churning hot air and driving dust
into pores, through hair,
swirling up into noses
and scouring throats?

After your clothes were washed,
Mum scrubbing hard at the stains,
Dad repeated over and over,
'They were prize birds,
not just any old eggs!'
with Mum's coda:
'Prize birds or no prize birds
you shouldn't have done it.'

You still fear the moment
when you reached down
and grabbed a handful of those
beautiful and delicate eggs –
ignoring the frantic quails at your feet –
and hurled them at your brother
without knowing why.
You can't forget. And he
can't forget his reply.

Reclamation

1 *Probable Sensations*

Nights on St George's beach,
camped under an upturned boat,
the drag marks gouged into cold sand
reaching up above the mark
of high tide, fishing and diving gear
the armaments of semi-itinerancy,
a hunter-gatherer parody,
declaration of independence,
the tailor running fast with razor
teeth, crayfish bristling below
the reef, a bottle of green ginger
wine burning your insides out,
occluding sleep. Compilation
of a video-memory, to which
probable sensations
are applied at a later date: that
below the boat, close with the breath
of your mates, you felt your skin prickle
with fear, despite the alcohol,
despite the anonymity of the sea.

2 *Front Beach*

Down in front of the Sail-Inn
the Bogs – decked out in black jeans, black t-shirts,
and black ripple-soled desert boots –
would take to the 'Abos'
with knives and clubs. Sometimes
the deckies would roll into town
and 'beat the shit
out of the lot of them...'
the thin arc of Front Beach:
annotation to a race riot.

3 *Blue Poles*

A print of Pollock's *Blue Poles*
hung in the school stairwell.
Tony Bellotti, about to thump
'Dictionary', just for the hell of it,
was disarmed by the question
'Hey, what do you reckon
this picture's all about?'
Fist mid-air, he replied, 'I don't know
but I wonder every time
I walk past. It always gives me the feeling
that something's trying to escape.
You know what I mean?'

4 *Disjunction*

It wasn't so much that she *had to watch*
but that she laughed until the blood
filled her face like a balloon,
that she laughed again
as she spoke of it
in the cool of the evening –
that a chook dancing
round the back garden
its lopped head dumb on the block
was the funniest thing she'd ever seen;
that she told you again under the covers
when you touched each other
with nervous fingers, the blood
hot and fast
in your twitching bodies.

5 *The Debate*

'War as population control'
had the Head Girl so riled up
that she skipped her prepared speech
and got stuck into them instead.
One of the guys on the other team,

flushed with victory, said later:
'She got really hot! Her dress
rode up her legs. Her knickers
were as red as her face.'

6 *Chapman River, where...*

The off-colour of the water
in summer, the influx of the sea when the sandbar
broke through in winter. The sandstone cliffs
upstream where the river ate through history
and ignored settlement. Where human nature
was a sack of cats dumped down on the flats
below by persons unknown, driving a blue car
with covered number plates. Where an army reserve
backed onto the gorge, and you considered that
despite live ammunition nature had the best chance
behind the barbed-wire. Where bream grew smarter
along the lengths of a golf course, dragging red flesh
on endless runs, poisoning the unwitting
with their spikes. Where heat and water birds colluded
and something like myth made a ghost of itself
and got into your bones. When solitude
became reason enough for fear and the city
hundreds of miles South was always too close.

7 *Identification*

How could you identify them when your face was a sticky pulp?
Later, they said *it's a good thing your glasses broke.*

8 *Greenough River*

Where really big fish would get trapped
when the rivermouth closed over.
A bit loose, the families that lived there.
Their yards unfenced.
The hamlet up-river as old
as settlement could get. Trees

took the wind into their veins, warped
and bent, and carrying a resentment
that made for popular postcards.

9 *The girl who shot the cop*

Remember the girl who couldn't cope
with the idea that some high-speed cop
had chased her boyfriend
to his death

who also shot at
the ambulance officers
as they came to pull her bleeding
cop out of the gutter.

Her sister returned to school
looking smaller than usual;
the teachers took her aside,
spoke quietly to her.

One of them told the class
he could understand
taking a gun to the world. The rest
of the town said bring back the rope.

When you got your licence
the guys made you drive
to the T-junction where the boyfriend had
wiped out. That cop used to make

a point of hanging out down there,
waiting for smart arses
who'd just got cars,
who might want to size up

the glint of his sunglasses,
the power of his Ford V8,
his ability to keep it together
when the pressure was on.

Parallels *(with Tracy Ryan)*
(for Dorothy Hewett in celebration of her 75th birthday)

1

The temperature is rising
and the folks here are pretending
its bordering on a heatwave;
the *Independent*'s World Weather
says it's 19 in Sydney so heading
into winter you're a borderline case:
the mercury is a cultural register!
And back in Perth where we share
the river and peculiar freedom
that comes with a parallel
Mediterranean climate,
it is the same, as moving
into early evening
the sun extends its heat,
where we assume
an apogee.

2

Long gone
summers snap at the
heels like asphalt –
progress a lie, we are
encircled and never
get free however the day
strains and fails, the light
'not quite switched on',
even the faintest heat
an illumination, the poem
rendering present.

Abishag
(after Rilke)

1

She lay. And her child arms
were tied by servants around the withering man
on whom she lay the sweet long hours,
a little frightened before his fading.

And sometimes, when an owl screeched,
she turned her face in his beard,
and all that was night came crowding in
around her with desire and fear.

The stars trembled as if part of her,
a scent probed the bedchamber,
the curtain flickered like a sign,
her gaze following its message –

but she gripped the dark old man
and, untouched by the night of nights,
lay over his regal chill –
virginal and light as a soul.

2

The king sat brooding all the empty day
over past deeds and missed pleasures,
recalling his favourite bitch, which he pampered.
But in the evening Abishag
curved over him. His turbulent life lay
abandoned like a notorious coast
beneath the zodiac of her still breasts.

Occasionally, as an expert on women,
he recognised through his eyebrows
the unmoved, kissless mouth;
and saw: her passion's green wand
did not bend down to his core.
A chill struck. He strained like a dog,
on the scent of his own last blood.

Ode to John Forbes
(*or,* Ring of Bright Water)

The interior fights back
like the inoculated rabbit
in the Flinders Ranges
as you watch an adult movie
just to find that it doesn't
do the trick, despite a view
from the hotel window
out over the sweeping coast,
and summer fashions
in the bar that might be
pure Sydney. In Melbourne
you don't get as much of the beach
as you'd like and have probably
forgotten what bright water
really is; well, from Bondi
I write that Dupain's bathers
wear style like suncream,
and despite the risk
wear little else.
Consider the resilience
of the pastoral
in the management of guilt
in which diocesan support
helps you through such
difficult times: when drought comes
or the wool prices are down
they improvise, live off their wits;
and despite the concentration
of the population on the edge
they still look inwards
when fluctuating prices
upset the budget –
those yokels from Ironbark
need a city bloke like you
to put them in their places!

And in that crucible of post-modernity,
where you helped invent the
'Sydney Poem', they forget
the immediacy of nostalgia
that wasn't borrowed
from the post-atomic 50s,
or the belief that it was
the Americans who led
the coasties away
from the grim idyll
of the interior.
The challenge for an
Aussie otter is to glow
like neon on the balmiest
evening, to swim in company
in the unsublime waters
of the Harbour
listening to 'Good Vibrations'
as container loads
of manufactured goods
make their way towards
the centre of the Empire.

Conflated Memories: a list

(for John Forbes)

On Hilton stationery
the streets of San Francisco
are a jetlagged schematic
of recall and heart-crunching
gradients, hesitation
before lunging momentum –
it's for you, this poem
I couldn't write in Cambridge –
here where Trans-ams
and Rancheros agitate at crossroads
like martinis shaken, not stirred,
where the corner of Mason and Geary
brings in the New Year
and riot police incite
revellers to infamy;
homeless and living with aids
a gentle tremor is felt
and Metallica plan a pas de deux
with the San Francisco
Symphony Orchestra.
In Borders every tree is a book,
in Macy's every shopping bag therapy;
newspaper vending machines convolute
on Market Street – safety in numbers,
multi-lingual, polymorphous,
earthquake-tolerant highrise culture,
rental cars, phone cards,
massages, all nomenclature
just off Union Square,
irony bobbing like toe-tags off The Rock,
valet parking as glitzy as you'd expect.
In the King Deli a Bud sign flickers
not with uncertainty but confidence,
knowing, and knowing
so rapidly, saying
'the military has left the Presidium –
a few buildings and a strategic

array of views reminds
us it was there' – and the bit
you'd have liked best,
keeping up the history
in case you might decide
to believe in God:
the God of Grace, the God of
the First Church of Christ, Scientist,
Pacific Heights, the God
of imported European Cars
and a burgeoning economy,
the God that brought down the Alamo
somewhere else, CNN reports
of further strikes in the Gulf,
loveless rooms floating
with seismic confidence.

Funeral Oration

(for Joyce Heywood)

The grave is a gate you send flowers through,
and the pink blossom frosting the northern hemisphere
is, on closer observation, a confluence of species.
There is a scent that's as much about lingering
as leaving, and it's about time the ploughs
were moving down there. The geographical
centre fluctuates while the magnetic centre
remains rock solid. Prayer goes somewhere
and is not lost and expects nothing back.
An old tree – a York Gum – oozes sap
like it's something special in this genealogy.
Most of the family is there and words are said
and those who can't attend wait for news of the dead
   as now it is all about memory.

Cranach's Venus Wows Them on the Catwalks of New York

Maybe it's the perfect combination of prêt-à-porter
and haute couture, a one-off creation that suggests
it's just off the rack, that any woman can wear;
and the punters saying 'it's just so 1990s,
who'd think they'd be so liberated?'
as if they're the only ones who might live
outside of history, who can pick and choose
from whichever era they fancy, like state
executioners or sadists, the model
perfectly out of tune with the actualities
of the body, insisting on the creator's
image, where the wilds of the accompanying
music solidify into the primal forest,
where spirits would ambush progress
like viruses whose cures evaporate
with their discovery, as brightly lit
as the glass of skyscrapers
almost reflected in the Hudson,
or an electric halo burning blood,
and the critics deciding
that Venus – supermodel's supermodel –
would have looked doubly tempting,
even risqué and taboo-ridden,
in a heavy sackcloth suit, as if
she mattered.

Love Poem

A pair of foxes
lie in death together
untouched by the hunter:
an expression
of devotion –
reductio ad absurdum –
like the poor dog
starving on the grave
of its master – held up
as human virtue
in an animal.
A crop duster crazy
in its dives over the hill
affects longevity,
silently we share
a strange sort of destiny.
A pair of foxes lying
on straw in a deserted pig shed
probably dined
on strychnine – a stimulant,
an analogy for love.

Reversal

*'In the decade that followed Aboriginal labour, forced and free, proved a
boon at York during the wheat harvest and many crops would have rotted
in fields without their help. The use of Aboriginal police constables in the
1840s guaranteed the settlers a trouble-free district. The resistance of the
York Nyungars was at an end; their numbers declined, their strength was
sapped, their people dispossessed, their vital harmony with their land and
the Dreaming irreparably shattered.'*

NEVILLE GREEN, *Broken Spears:
Aboriginals and Europeans in the southwest of Australia*

Recollection works as backdrop
and anchors image: the haze,
waves of heat that stretch out
across denuded hills,
gentle folds rock-picked
and cut to the quick, stookers
having a bite to eat under York Gums
by the top gate, car doors wide open
and a waterbag passed around.
A Nyungar family
from the fringe of town.
An articulation
across a fragmenting line,
Needlings stark in the background,
driving slowly past
watching each other vanish,
the city uneasy in the south.
Thirty years back. Reconfigure –
scrub, sound of truck, layout.
It's just a picture, a glimpse
that brought emotions
lost to childhood
in a district of faults
and crevices. Early settlers
garnished kitchens with ears
of murdered Nyungars:
they fear the spirits of their dead.
Knowing the heat
each stalk of wheat
holds in itself: the colour

of florescence. It is language
that contracts. Its growth, illusory.
A sign appears on the rust road:
    SHEEP CROSSING.
Harvest done, coronas mark fields –
seen and heard by none,
the season turned upside down.